COUNTRY INSIGHTS

INDIA

David Cumming

HODDER
Wayland

an imprint of Hodder Children's Books

COUNTRY INSIGHTS

BRAZIL • CHINA • CZECH REPUBLIC • DENMARK • FRANCE
INDIA • JAPAN • KENYA

For more information on this series and other Hodder Wayland titles, go to www.hodderwayland.co.uk

GUIDE TO THIS BOOK

 As well as telling you about the whole of India, this book looks closely at the city of Bangalore and the village of Thrickodithanam.

This city symbol will appear at the top of the page and information boxes each time the book looks at Bangalore.

 This rural symbol will appear each time the book looks at Thrickodithanam.

Cover photograph: A group of children in India.

Title page: Two boys having fun at the seaside with their father.

Contents page: Women and children in Rajasthan's traditionally bright clothing, in the Thar Desert, north-west India.

Book editor: Alison Cooper
Series editor: Polly Goodman
Book designer: Mark Whitchurch
Series designer: Tim Mayer
Consultant: Anne Marley, Principal Librarian, Children and Schools Library Service for Hampshire.

First published in 1997 by Wayland Publishers Ltd

Revised and updated in 2006 by Hodder Wayland, an imprint of Hodder Children's Books

© Copyright 1997 Hodder Wayland

British Library Cataloguing in Publication Data
Cumming, David
  India. – (Country Insights)
  1. India – Social conditions – Juvenile literature
  I. Title
  954'.052

ISBN-10: 0750248238
ISBN-13: 9780750248235

Picture acknowledgements
All photographs are by David Cumming.
Map artwork is by Hardlines.
Border artwork is by Kate Davenport.

Typeset by Mark Whitchurch, England.
Printed in China

Hodder Children's Books
A division of Hodder Headline Limited
338 Euston Road, London NW1 3BH

Contents

Introducing India

As you travel through India, everything keeps changing – the scenery, the people, the food, the languages. This is why India is often described as not one country, but a collection of countries. Travelling from the north to the south is like crossing a continent. India is the world's second most-crowded country, home to sixteen out of every hundred people on this planet. Only neighbouring China contains more people.

The story of modern India really begins in 1947. The British had ruled India as a colony for over 200 years, but in 1947, the country finally gained its independence again.

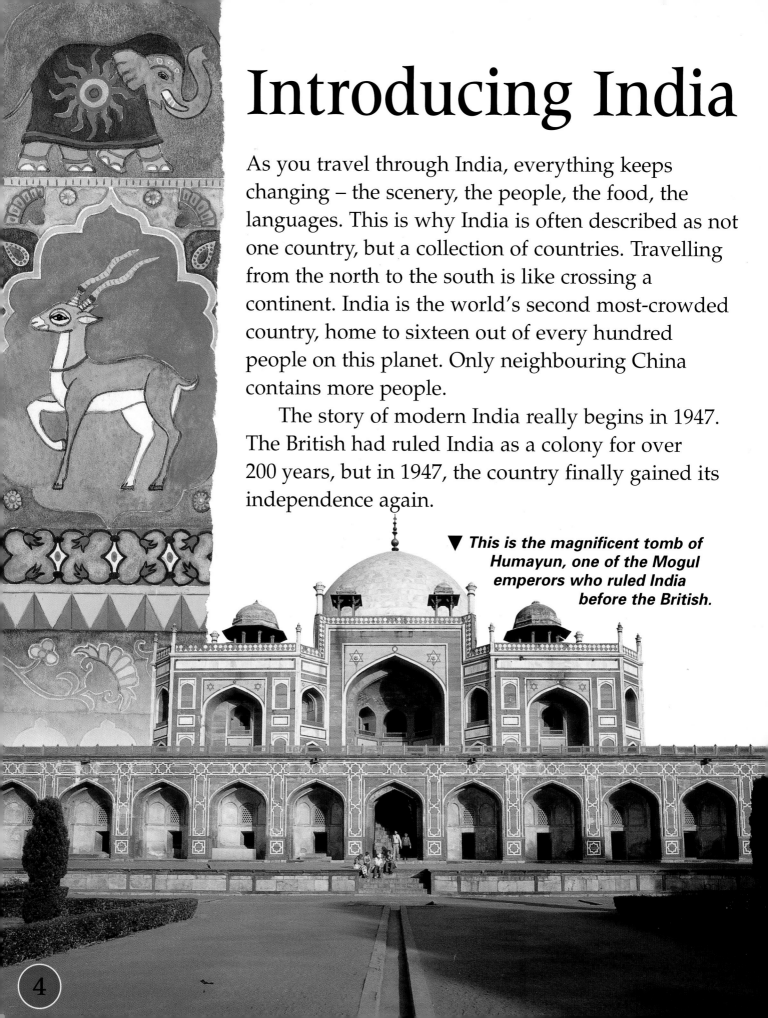

▼ *This is the magnificent tomb of Humayun, one of the Mogul emperors who ruled India before the British.*

The years of British rule had done a lot of harm. Instead of industrializing and becoming wealthier, as countries in Europe had done, India had slipped backwards. There were hundreds of millions of Indians who could neither read nor write. They had little money and not enough food.

Since 1947, India has done a lot of catching up. It is now one of the most industrialized countries in the world. But the wealth this has created has not been shared equally. Today, there is a big gap between the 'rich' cities and the 'poor' villages, which the government is trying to close.

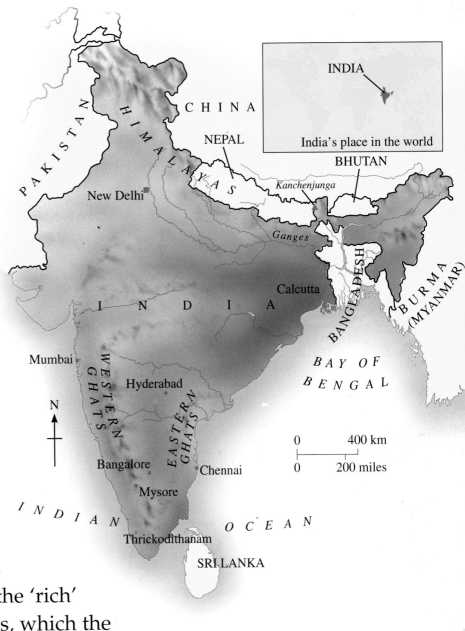

INDIA FACTS

Total land area:	3,287,263 km²
Highest point:	Kanchenjunga (8,598 m)
Longest river:	Ganges (2,655 km)
Population:	1.08 billion
Capital:	New Delhi
Main languages:	Hindi and English
Currency:	Indian rupee

▲ This book will take you to the city of Bangalore and to the village of Thrickodithanam, as well as the rest of India. You can find these places on the map.

The city of Bangalore

In 1537, Kempe Gowda, a powerful chieftain, visited the boundary of his lands in southern India. He decided to build a fort there to keep his enemies out. 'One day,' he said, 'this little fort will be in the centre of a great city.' Kempe Gowda must have had a strange sense of humour, because he called this city Bengaluru (meaning 'boiled beans') after the meal he had just eaten. Today, the 'city of boiled beans' is known as Bangalore. It is the fifth-largest city in India.

BANGALORE FACTS

Area:	368 km²
Population:	6 million
Main languages:	English, Kannada and Hindi

▼ *These busy streets are in the old part of the city.*

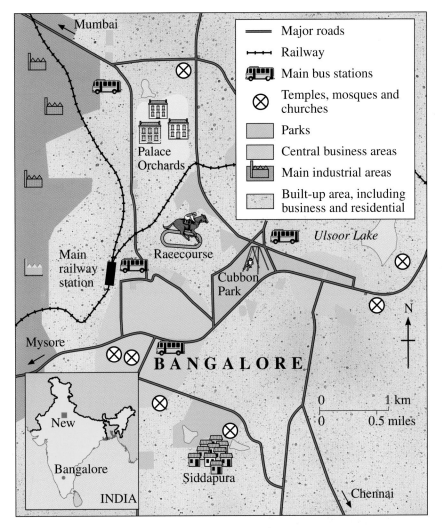

When the British ruled India, they used Bangalore as a base from which to control the southern part of the country. They constructed roads and railways for good communications. In the area of the city where their officials lived, they built wide, tree-lined roads, bungalows with big, well-kept gardens, and parks full of flowers. Soon, people began to talk about 'the garden city' and 'beautiful Bangalore'.

Sadly, much of this area has now been destroyed. Hotels, offices and blocks of flats have been built in its place, as the city has grown… and grown… and grown.

'The old part of the city is always busy with shoppers, so my hair bands sell well.' – Ravi Parthasarthy, stallholder (right).

Women in Bangalore ▶ buying hair bands from Ravi Parthasarthy's street stall.

A village in Kerala

The small state of Kerala stretches down the south-western tip of India. It is a narrow strip of land, sandwiched between the warm waters of the Arabian Sea and the forested slopes of the highlands. Nearly 75 per cent of Keralans live in the countryside, in villages like Thrickodithanam.

VILLAGE FACTS

Area:	10 km²
Population:	275
Main language:	Malayalam

The village of Thrickodithanam is spread out among fields and forests. Its forty houses, and other buildings, are linked by earth paths or uneven stone tracks. The village has a few shops, which sell meat, fruit and vegetables, and everyday things like soap.

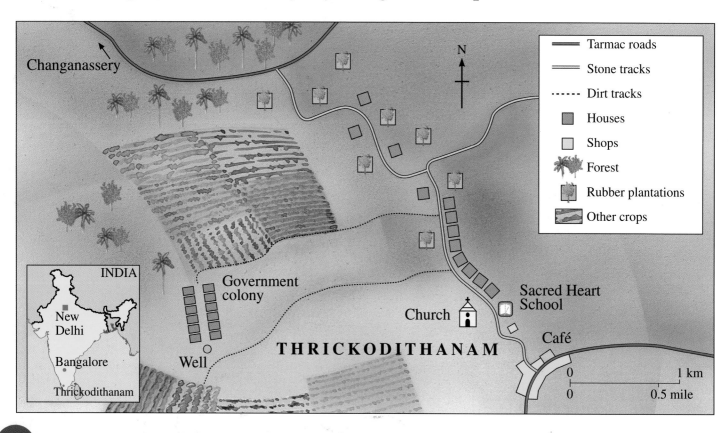

There is also a school, a church and a meeting-hall. By the side of the meeting-hall, there is a tiny room that a doctor uses once a week to treat the sick with natural medicines. Villagers who are seriously ill have to be taken to the hospital in the nearest town, Changanassery, which is 10 km away.

The Government Colony is in the heart of Thrickodithanam. This is a group of twenty-two houses built close together on either side of an earth track. The people who live there are the poorest in the village. They are so poor that the government has had to help them by providing land cheaply and lending them money to build their homes.

▲ These women and children live in the Government Colony.

'This is a lovely place to live. We can play all day in the forests and fields.' – Sanely, 12 years old (right).

Twelve-year-old Sanely ▶ looking after her two-year-old brother, Jewell.

Land and climate

The Himalayas, the world's highest mountains, extend for 2,500 km across the north of India. Just south of the Himalayas, the land is very flat. Most of India's population live in this area because plenty of food can be grown here. The soil is rich, and the River Ganges provides water.

The Deccan Plateau takes up much of southern India. It is an area of flat-topped high ground, very different from the spiky peaks of the Himalayas. Hills called the Western Ghats and the Eastern Ghats poke out on each side of the Deccan Plateau and slope down to the coast.

▼ *Terraced fields lie around tiny villages high up in the Himalayas. The Himalayas cut off India from the rest of the Asian continent.*

▲*Women in the Thar Desert. Their scarves are traditional dress, but they also help to protect against the hot sun and dry dust of the desert.*

India has three seasons – hot, wet and cool. From February to May, it is the hot season. On the plains of the River Ganges, temperatures often soar to a baking 50 °C. Temperatures become more comfortable during the wet season, which lasts from June until November. Most of India receives rain then, with some parts getting much more than others.

Between December and mid-February, India is at its driest and coolest. Up in the Himalayas, of course, it is always cold, but even along the Ganges river, the nights are chilly at this time of year.

Since it is near the Equator, temperatures in the south of India vary little, hovering around 30 °C all year: in the hot season it is a few degrees higher, and in the cool season a few degrees lower.

THE MONSOON

'Monsoon' is the name of the wind that brings rain to India. Between June and September, it blows across India from the south-west. In October, it changes direction and blows from the north-east. The monsoon is very important to India's farmers, who need the rain it brings to make their crops grow. In some years, the monsoon brings a lot of rain and floods occur. In other years, there is very little rain, and crops and animals die.

Mawsynram in north-east India is one of the wettest places on earth. It receives 11,873 mm of rain a year. It rains there about 147 days every year.

A pleasant climate

The British liked living in Bangalore because of its pleasant climate. It is neither too hot nor too cold. Bangalore is situated on top of the Deccan Plateau, 920 m above sea-level. Because it is higher up, it is always cooler during the hot season than cities nearer sea-level.

The lowest temperatures occur between November and February. At this time of year, the evenings and early mornings can be chilly. The people of Bangalore often wake up to a city covered in thick fog during these cool months.

The hottest part of the year is from March to the end of May, when temperatures can climb to 35 °C in the daytime. Fans and air-conditioners are switched on at full power to make homes and offices more bearable.

'I like December and January best because I can ride my bike around all day. Just before the monsoon comes it's too hot to go outside.' – Sadiq, 10 years old (left).

▲ *Ulsoor Lake is 1.5 km². It stores water for the city, for use in the dry months at the start of each year.*

BANGALORE'S CLIMATE	
Average rainfall:	940 mm per year
Average minimum temperature:	15°C (January)
Average maximum temperature:	33 °C (April)

Everyone breathes a huge sigh of relief at the end of May. They know that the south-west monsoon will arrive soon and lower the high temperatures. From June to September this wind brings rain to the city every day. Most of it falls in a single, long burst between 4 and 7 pm. The heaviest rains, though, are brought by the north-east monsoon in October and November. For the rest of the year (December–May), Bangalore is dry.

A wide variety of fruit and ▶ vegetables is grown in the countryside around Bangalore and sold in the markets.

Green and hot

The villagers of Thrickodithanam tell visitors that anything will grow in their land. 'Push a walking-stick into it,' they laugh, 'and in a year you will have a tree!' While this may be a joke, it is certainly true that Thrickodithanam is very green, like the rest of the state of Kerala. Every bit of land seems to have something growing in it, whether it is a coconut or rubber tree, a pineapple plant or a row of vegetables.

THE VILLAGE'S CLIMATE	
Average rainfall:	153 mm per year
Average minimum temperature:	22°C (December–January)
Average maximum temperature:	33°C (March)

The village farmers are helped by the climate and the rich soil. There is plenty of sunshine, and it is hot all year round, with the temperature only dropping to 20 °C during the cool nights of December and January. There is rain all year round too, unlike other parts of India. The heaviest rain is brought by the south-west monsoon, with about 300 mm falling in June alone. Less rain is brought at the end of the year by the north-east monsoon.

▼ *The state of Kerala is criss-crossed by rivers, which provide water for farmers and are useful for transport.*

'We get hot and sweaty in this heat, so we have to drink lots of tea and water while we are working.' – Isaac Pathrose, stonemason (below, left).

Home life

All over India, people's lives are centred on the home and family. Village people usually have large families so that their children can help in the fields. In the cities, most parents now have only one or two children, because the government is trying to reduce the number of babies being born.

All Indian children are taught to respect their elders and to pay attention to what they say. Parents like to keep an eye on their children, so sons and daughters are not encouraged to leave home. Even newly married couples continue to live with one partner's parents. One reason for this is that there is a shortage of housing. But it is also because the parents do not like to see their children leaving home and the family splitting up. Often, grandparents, aunts and uncles share the family home too.

◀ *For parents living in the city, it is not so important to have lots of children to help with the work. Many, like the man travelling on this rickshaw, have only two children.*

16

HOME COOKING

Hinduism discourages the eating of meat, so most Indians are vegetarians. A *thali* is a meal eaten in homes all over India. It is named after the metal tray on which it is served. There will be a heap of rice in the centre of the *thali*, surrounded by several bowls.

These might contain *dhal* (lentil gravy), yoghurt, *mattar panir* (cheese and peas in a spicy sauce), *aalu gobi* (cauliflower and potato), or a variety of other vegetable mixtures.

Chapatis, which are like thin pancakes, pickles and chutneys will also be on the *thali*.

▼ *These workers are enjoying a* thali *meal during their lunch-hour. Indians always pick up their food with their fingers.*

Most Indians follow Hinduism as a religion. Their homes usually have a shrine, around which the family gathers every day to worship. There are also Indians who are Muslims, Christians, Sikhs and Buddhists. Whatever their faith, religion is part of daily life for people all over India.

▼ *A Hindu family visiting a holy place on the Ganges river. Three of the women are using their scarves to hide their faces because they are shy.*

17

Home life in Bangalore

Like all cities in India, Bangalore has a mixture of rich and poor people. Only the rich can afford to live in an area like Palace Orchards. Here, the streets are clean and wide, and the houses are big, new and full of expensive furniture. Each is protected by high walls and a guard at the gates. Every family has two or three servants, including a driver for their car.

▲ **The houses in Palace Orchards are some of the biggest and most expensive in the whole of the city.**

▼ **About a dozen or more families in Siddapura are crammed into the space taken up by just one family in Palace Orchards.**

The servants probably live in a part of Bangalore like Siddapura. Siddapura is called a 'slum' because hundreds of families are crammed into a very small area. The tiny one- or two-roomed houses have front doors opening right on to the street. Inside, the homes are furnished with only the bare essentials, for there is little money for any household luxuries.

Dev Peter, his wife Shylaja, and their two daughters, Shirlyn and Marlyn, consider themselves a typical, middle-class family, who are neither rich nor poor. They live in a modern two-floored, six-roomed house, with Dev's elderly parents. Dev and Shylaja have comfortable furniture and a new music system, video-recorder and colour television. Recently, they bought some land in another part of the city, and they are saving money so that they can build a new home there.

▼ *The Peter family enjoying a Sunday lunch of curried chicken, rice with spiced vegetables and salad.*

Country homes

Just as in Bangalore, the houses in Thrickodithanam show how rich their owners are. The house of the James family is one of the biggest and best. It has two floors. Downstairs, there is a large dining-room and kitchen, and a lounge with two bedrooms leading off it. Upstairs, there are another two bedrooms. The house has electricity and running water, and bottled gas is used for cooking. The family has a colour television and one of the few telephones in the village. They also have a walled garden.

In contrast, the families in the Colony have very simple homes, with just one or two rooms. Some of them are made of planks of wood, or palm leaves woven together. All the families have to fetch their water from the well in the village. Most of the houses have electricity, but only a few families have a television.

None of the people in the ▶ Colony have the money to build a good house.

20

In Thrickodithanam, all the members of a family like to live close together, so that they can help one another if someone is sick or very busy. José Chacko's sister and his wife's two brothers have built houses next to his. This means that no one is ever lonely, and there is always someone to share doing things like looking after the children.

▲ *A villager washing her cow in a stream. Most families own a cow. Some also have goats and chickens.*

'This is my kitchen. I've got a few pots and pans and some storage jars. I use wood to cook on.' – Remya, housewife (below).

India at work

Since almost 75 per cent of its people live in the countryside, it is not surprising that farming is the most important job in India. Working on the land is a tough job, and in India it is made more difficult by the climate. The farmers rely on the monsoon to water their crops. If it fails to bring enough, then they are in trouble. But they also have problems when the monsoon brings too much rain and their fields are flooded. In recent years, many farmers have given up battling with the climate and have headed for the cities, in search of an easier way to earn a living.

The British built few factories during the time that they ruled India. Although many have been built since 1947, there are still not enough to provide jobs for all the people who want to work in the cities. Many people who move from the villages to the cities end up with no work and a miserable life. The luckier ones might be able to find a part-time job, perhaps working in a hotel or a restaurant for a few days a month. A few learn a craft, such as mending shoes or umbrellas, and set up business on a street corner.

◀ *The climate is not the only problem farmers face. This farmer is spraying chemicals to stop pests eating his crop.*

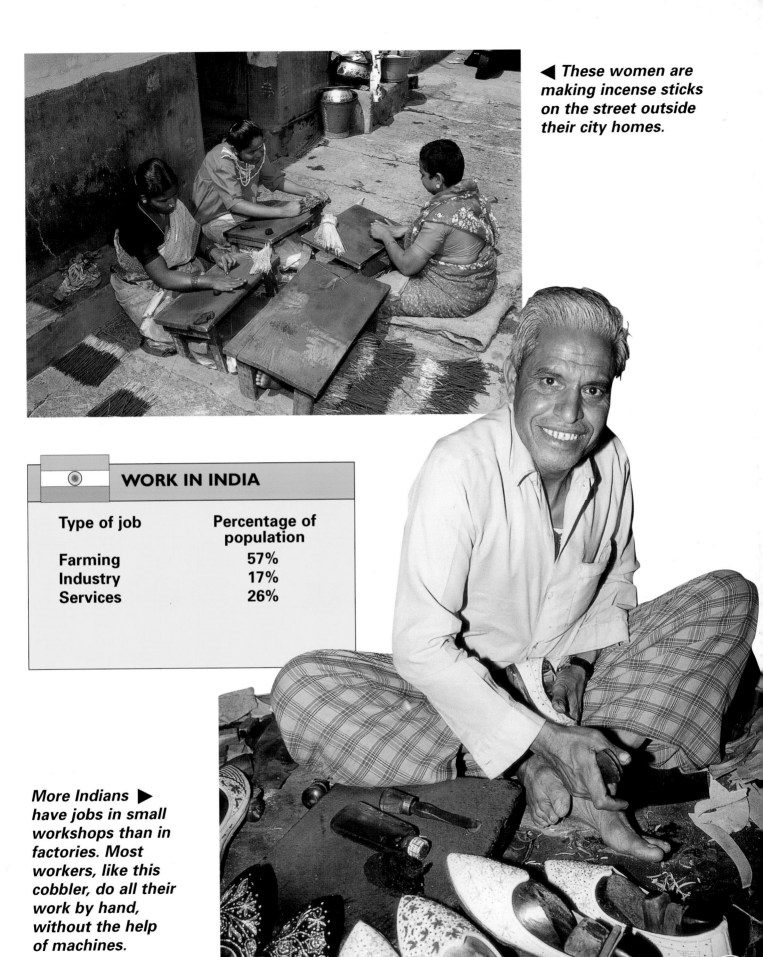

◄ These women are making incense sticks on the street outside their city homes.

WORK IN INDIA	
Type of job	**Percentage of population**
Farming	57%
Industry	17%
Services	26%

More Indians ► have jobs in small workshops than in factories. Most workers, like this cobbler, do all their work by hand, without the help of machines.

'Silicon city'

Bangalore is a fascinating mixture of the old and the new, and this is also true of the work opportunities available to the people who live there.

Thanks to the roads and railways built by the British, many industries have been attracted to the city since Independence in 1947. The good transport links have made it easy for businesses to bring raw materials to their factories and take the finished goods away to be sold. As a result, Bangalore has developed into one of India's main manufacturing cities. Aircraft, tools for machines, telephones, radios, clothes, shoes, watches and food are just some of the many things made there.

Recently, the city has become the main centre in India for computers. There are many firms here that write computer programs, as well as firms that assemble the computers. Today, the people of Bangalore joke that they can make anything from a potato chip to a silicon chip!

◀ *Bangalore has many skilled workers. This man works for a small engineering business, making parts for factory machines.*

There are many people in Bangalore who do more traditional jobs. Often, they are employed in small workshops owned by their families, using skills that they have been taught by their parents or relations. They do jobs such as repairing broken-down motorbikes and mopeds, or making the silk for which the city is famous.

CHILD WORKERS

In Bangalore, many children work instead of going to school, because their families are so poor. The children's employers make them work long hours for little pay. It is estimated that there are between 60 million and 115 million child workers in India. The government has passed new laws to reduce the number of child workers, and has opened shelters to help children who live in poverty on city streets.

'I've been working on this silk loom for the last three years. Having small hands means that I work much quicker than a grown-up.' Arun, 10 years old (right).

Village work

The people of Thrickodithanam earn a living in a variety of ways. Several of the wealthier families have bought land and planted rubber trees. Looking after these trees provides work for many of the other villagers.

▼ José Chacko collects latex from a rubber tree by slicing the bark with a special tool, and then collecting the sap in a coconut shell.

The James family have 500 rubber trees, and they employ José Chacko as a tapper. He comes every morning to collect the runny latex that oozes out of the bark of the trees. Then he mixes the latex with water and acid, and it turns into solid rubber overnight. The James family sells the rubber to factories in Changanassery, which turn it into door mats. Mr James works in Changanassery as the manager of a restaurant, so he does not have time to make rubber himself.

'I've been a rubber tapper for forty years, so I know what I'm doing and work fast. People say I'm the best in the area!' – José Chacko, 53 years old (left).

In the Colony area of Thrickodithanam, twenty-year-old Nazeer runs a small catering business with his father. They specialize in cooking food for weddings. A few doors along from Nazeer, Shias has an auto-rickshaw taxi that people can hire for journeys around Changanassery.

▲ Shias drives this auto-rickshaw taxi around Changanassery. He works every day from 8 am to 8 pm, except on Sundays, when he finishes at 5 pm and then goes to the cinema.

Most of Thrickodithanam's families own land. The smaller landowners use it to grow food for their families. Those with more land can produce crops to sell. They grow fruit and vegetables, such as tomatoes, onions, papayas and mangoes, and sell them locally, or in the weekly market in Changanassery.

Anand is employed ▶ by a large landowner to look after his crops in the fields next to the village.

Going to school

In India, all children are supposed to go to school between the ages of six and fourteen. In fact, many children stay away from their lessons, and relatively few complete eight years of full-time schooling. For example, 20 out of every 100 pupils drop out before they finish primary school.

One reason for this is that the government has not built enough schools. In the countryside, especially, the nearest school can be a long way away. Many families do not own a car or bike, and bus services are few and far between. This can make it very difficult for young children to get to school. On top of all these problems, if the children's parents never went to school, then they probably will not encourage their children to go.

SCHOOLS IN INDIA	
	Number of students
Primary schools	114 million
Middle schools	43 million
Secondary schools	27 million
Total	184 million

◀ *These city children go to and from their school in an auto-rickshaw taxi. The fare is cheap because so many of them travel in it!*

Poverty is another reason why children do not go to school. Many Indian families are so poor that earning money is considered more important than learning. They prefer to send their children to work rather than to school.

▲ *There is no money for this country school to have a classroom, so lessons have to be held outside, even when it is cold.*

There is little equality between men and women in India. Men are usually expected to earn the family's money by working. Women are usually expected to stay at home and look after the children. As a result, many parents think that educating a daughter is a waste of time. They say it is far better for her to stay at home and learn about home life by helping her mother.

Children from richer families do usually complete their schooling. They live near good schools, and their parents encourage them to pass their exams, so that they can get good jobs.

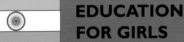 **EDUCATION FOR GIRLS**

In 2001, 54 per cent of females could not read or write.

The number of girls attending primary schools is growing though, and they now make up 44% of the total number of students enrolled in primary education.

School in Bangalore

Children who live in a city stand the best chance of getting a good education in India. In Bangalore, children with wealthy parents can go to one of the top private schools, such as Bishop Cotton's School or the Cathedral School, where fees have to be paid. The private schools can afford to pay high salaries to attract good teachers. They also have much better facilities than the government schools.

The government schools are free, but they do not provide as good an education as the private schools. Their teachers are not as well qualified, they have little equipment, and the classrooms are rundown. But poor families have little choice: it is either a government school or nothing.

▼ *At the Cathedral School, children learn to use computers from an early age.*

Classes start at 9 am and continue until 1 pm, with a short break mid-morning. They continue after lunch for the older pupils. Most children bring their own lunches to school – perhaps two or three *chapatis*, rice and some mixed vegetables. School finishes at 3.30 pm, when children can be seen squeezing into rickshaws or buses to be taken home.

When they leave school, pupils have a wide choice of places to continue their studies in Bangalore. There is a university, two medical schools and many colleges, where they can study subjects such as engineering and business management.

'We have to wear a uniform, like all schoolchildren in India. I'm going to be in trouble because I've lost my tie.' – Ashok, pupil at Cathedral School, 11 years old (below, centre).

A country school

The Sacred Heart School is the only school in Thrickodithanam. This primary school is attended by 330 girls and boys, aged between three-and-a-half and eleven years old. Although it is run by Roman Catholics, children from other religions are welcome there. Pupils come from all the surrounding villages. The older ones walk to school, and for some this is a walk of up to 5 km. The younger ones are brought on the family motorbike or bicycle.

This school has little money. As a result, there is no electricity, and the classrooms are bare, apart from a few posters and drawings pinned to the walls. The classes are large, often with thirty-five children to a room.

All the teachers are women, and they teach in Malayalam, which is the main language of Kerala. The children also learn English, along with maths, geography and history.

'I walk to school every day in my bare feet. My favourite subjects are Malayalam, maths and social studies.' – Bincy, 10 years old (left).

Five-year-old pupils ▶
in their classroom
at the Sacred Heart
School.

If children want to continue their education after leaving the Sacred Heart School, they have to go to a secondary school in Changanassery. Then they can go to the college in the town. But if they want to study a subject that is not taught at the college, they have to go to the university in Kochi, which is three hours away by bus.

▼ *The children at the*
Sacred Heart School
play on this slide at
break-times.

India at play

There are many religions in India, which means that hardly a month goes by without a holiday or festival in honour of a saint or religious event. The biggest festival is Diwali, which lasts five days. Although it is special to Hindus, it is celebrated by everyone. It is similar to the Christian festival of Christmas, because it is a time for having parties, giving presents and decorating houses with lights.

Many Indians are cinema-goers, and India makes more new films than anywhere else in the world. In 2001, India made 1,013 films. The city of Mumbai, known until 1995 as Bombay, has even been nicknamed 'Bollywood', because the film industry is as important there as it is in Hollywood in the USA.

MAJOR FESTIVALS AND HOLIDAYS IN INDIA	
1 Jan	New Year's Day (national holiday)
mid-Jan	Pongal (Hindu)
26 Jan	Republic Day (national holiday)
Jan–Feb	Ramadan and Eid-ul-Fitr (Muslim)
Feb–Mar	Holi (Hindu)
April	Baisakhi (Sikh)
June	Buddha Jayanti (Buddhist)
15 Aug	Independence Day (national holiday)
Oct	Dussehra (Hindu)
Nov	Diwali (Hindu)
25 Dec	Christmas Day (Christian)

Diwali is the Hindu ▶ 'festival of lights', when streets and shops are decorated with lights and banners.

Indian films are a mixture of singing, dancing and fighting, with the 'goodie' always defeating the 'baddie' in the end. Indian film stars are among the richest people in India, and many go on to become powerful politicians.

▲ *A family playing on a beach. The parents are wearing clothes because most Indians do not like showing their bodies in public.*

Indians also enjoy sports. Cricket is by far the most popular game. When an important match is being played, ears are glued to radios, and

	TELEVISIONS AND TELEPHONES IN INDIA
	The number of televisions and telephones is rising in India, but there are still relatively few. Just over 30% of households own a television, while only around 9% have a telephone.

televisions are surrounded by crowds eager to know the score. Loud cheers greet victory; very glum faces reflect defeat. In streets and parks in all the towns and cities, children practise their batting and bowling in the hope that one day they will follow their heroes on to the pitch.

Leisure time in Bangalore

There are a lot of things for people in Bangalore to see and do when they are not working. The city's pleasant climate makes it ideal for a variety of outdoor sports. There is a modern sports stadium, seven large, open-air swimming pools, two golf courses, lakes for boating, and clubs with tennis and squash courts and gyms. Bangalore is also famous as a centre for breeding and racing horses. The racecourse gets crowded at weekends, as people eagerly bet money on the horses they hope will win.

At weekends, many rich city people head for the surrounding countryside. Recently, holiday resorts have been opened there, with restaurants, indoor play areas, sports facilities and cottages to stay in. They have become very fashionable places to visit.

▼ *People can surf the internet at one of the city's cyber-cafes. India's first cyber-cafe opened in 1996.*

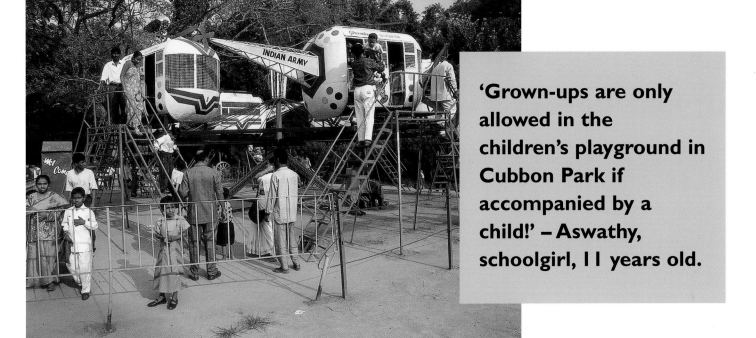

'Grown-ups are only allowed in the children's playground in Cubbon Park if accompanied by a child!' – Aswathy, schoolgirl, 11 years old.

▲ *Families go to Cubbon Park at the weekends for a walk, and to visit the playground or enjoy a funfair ride.*

Women are often ▶ *seen driving around Bangalore, although such behaviour would be frowned upon in many other parts of India.*

Back in Bangalore, there are many places to go if the weather is bad. India's second-largest aquarium is in Cubbon Park, and the city also has two interesting museums and a planetarium.

The people of Bangalore work hard, but they also tend to have an easy-going approach to life. Most do not object to people drinking alcohol, or to women driving, things that offend the majority of Indians. Their relaxed attitude is reflected in the number of bars and discos in the city. After work these places are crammed with people having a good time, and enjoying spending the money they have earned.

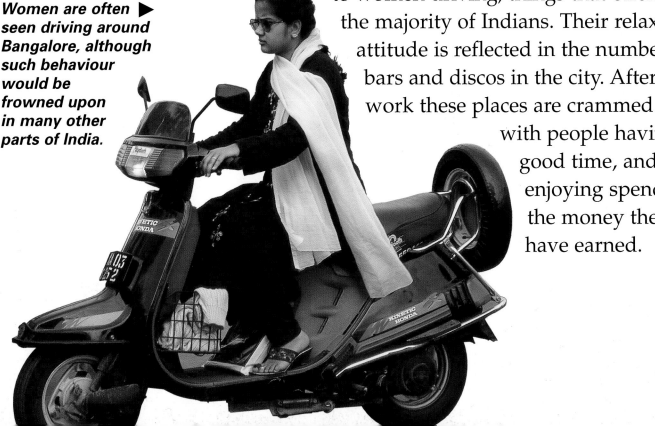

Village leisure

There are no bars, sports clubs or museums in Thrickodithanam, and the nearest cinema is in Changanassery, a bus journey away. The villagers have to amuse themselves. Children make toys from any odd bits and pieces that they can find lying about. They play football and cricket on any open space.

The women in the village turn their work into a social occasion. Often, their houses are close enough for them to chat with each other while they feed their animals or prepare meals. Then they go off to the well or stream to do their washing together. This helps to pass the time and makes their daily chores less boring. Needless to say, such togetherness means that news travels fast. There are few secrets in Thrickodithanam.

◀ *Nine-year-old Jino with the wheel rim he plays with.*

'I chase this old wheel rim around for hours. It's great fun. I've only hit one person with it today – my mother.'
– Jino, 9 years old (right).

A mid-morning break ▶ for a cup of coffee outside the village café. In southern India, people drink coffee, while in the north, tea is more popular.

In the evenings, families with televisions invite their neighbours in to watch a popular programme or film. This is also a time when the men are free to play cards or talk with their friends.

There is work to be done in the cool of the early morning, so few people stay up late. Weddings and festivals are the exception, of course. Then the singing and dancing, and fun and games can go on long into the night.

▼ Catching up on news about India and Kerala. The newspaper is written in Malayalam.

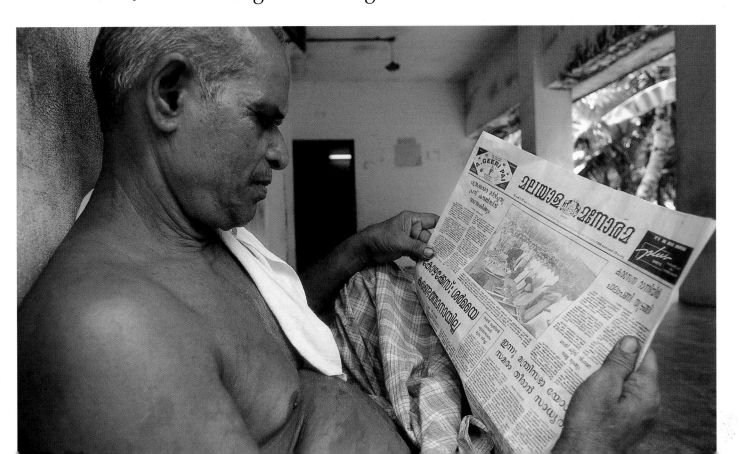

The future

After it became independent, India almost shut itself off from the world. After years of interference from the British, it wanted to be left alone to develop in the way it wanted.

India achieved a lot on its own. Today, there are many new industries. Its people are healthier than they were in 1947, and more of them can read and write. Yet much still has to be done so that the millions of poor Indians can have a better life. New factories and homes are required, as well as more schools and hospitals.

At the end of the 1980s, the government decided that India needed better links with other countries, to help it to modernize. Foreign companies were invited in to help India prepare for the next century. Indian firms began selling more products abroad.

▼ *Two European firms helped to build this expensive suspension bridge over the Hooghly river in Calcutta.*

With its doors open to the world, India was soon booming. There were more jobs. People had more money. There were more goods in the shops. It was as if India had been reborn. Here was a 'new' India, an India that would be much richer than the 'old' one.

In the recent rush to build new factories and buy new things, the poor have been forgotten. Although they are not worse off, they have not benefited as much as the rich, who have got richer. But this is just the beginning. The hope is that, within ten years, the new India will be able to help its poorer citizens. There will still be poor people, but far fewer than in the old India.

▲ Computerized banking is now available in the major cities.

INDIA'S PROGRESS, 1961–2001		
	1961	**2001**
Life expectancy	41 years	64 years
Percentage of total population who can read and write	24%	64%
Percentage of total population who are poor	55%	29%

Although many things ▶ have been modernized in India, traditional ways of life continue in country areas. These horse-drawn tongas are still used in some parts of India.

The future of Bangalore

▲ *Traffic jams and pollution are serious problems that need tackling before they get any worse.*

POPULATION GROWTH IN BANGALORE	
1951	786,000
1994	5.2 million
2005	6 million

Bangalore is one of the cities that has benefited most from the boom times brought by the 'new' India. New factories have created more jobs. People can now visit modern shopping malls and a large sports stadium. There is also a new airport where jumbo jets can land. It is one of the fastest-growing cities in the whole of Asia. Unfortunately, this rapid growth is causing many problems. The price of land has rocketed in the scramble to build homes for the city's new workers. Water, already in short supply, has to be rationed during the dry season. Power cuts are more common because power stations cannot keep up with the increased demand for electricity.

More people mean more traffic and more waste. Cars, buses and taxis jam the streets, their exhausts belching fumes. Rubbish is dumped everywhere because there are not enough refuse collectors to take it away. Bangalore is getting dirtier and more polluted by the month. It seems that the old 'garden city' of Bangalore, famous for its open spaces and fresh air, is disappearing.

Instead of looking back, the people of Bangalore need to look ahead and make the best of the new city. The local authorities are aware of all the problems, but they do not have enough money to tackle them. For example, they need to build new roads to reduce the traffic jams. However, the taxes being paid by the new businesses will give them the money to start cleaning up the city.

'Just like the city, my business has taken off in the past few years. There is certainly more money in Bangalore these days.'
– Dev Peter, businessman, (below).

Dev Peter's ▶ electrical company is one of many businesses that have benefited from the growth of Bangalore.

The village's future

Unlike Bangalore, little is expected to change in Thrickodithanam in the near future. The older villagers, though, are worried that more young people will move away. Neither the village nor nearby Changanassery has much to offer them. The recent changes in India are making the cities seem even more attractive than they did in the past, and not only because more jobs are available in them.

No one in Thrickodithanam has satellite television, but many young villagers have watched it at friends' homes in Changanassery. Television programmes are now beamed into Changanassery from all over the world. These, together with the new films from the USA on show in the cinema, are helping to make the teenagers restless. Many of them want a way of life like the ones they see in films or on television. Thrickodithanam cannot offer them such a life, but perhaps a city can.

▼ *Many of these village children will move away to one of India's cities in a few years' time.*

The poor people of the Colony are hoping that some of the 'new' India's wealth will trickle down to them. They look forward to the day when all their houses have electricity and perhaps even piped water. Once this would have been a dream. Today, the chances of it happening soon are very real.

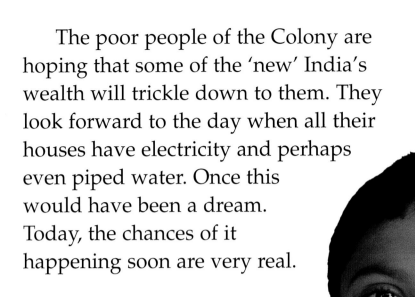

'My parents are paying for private lessons so that I can pass my exams and get a good job in a city.' – Jino, 10 years old (right).

▲ *Omana Kuttan is a skilled carpenter, as was his father. If his son does not follow in his footsteps, this traditional craft may die out in the village.*

Ten-year-old Jino ▶ *learning about India's cities in a geography lesson.*

Glossary

Auto-rickshaw taxi A small three-wheeled vehicle, powered by an engine, that can carry two or three passengers behind the driver.

Booming Becoming more successful.

Bungalows Houses built on one level, with no upstairs rooms.

Chapatis Flat pieces of bread, similar to pancakes.

Chieftain The leader of a group of people.

Climate The normal weather in a place.

Colony A country that is controlled by another country.

Continent A huge area of land containing many countries.

Currency The type of money used in a country.

Cycle-rickshaw taxi A small, three-wheeled vehicle, powered by a bicycle, that can carry two or three passengers behind the driver.

Equator An imaginary line around the centre of the earth, halfway between the North and South Poles.

Incense sticks Sticks that give off a perfume when they are burnt.

Independent A country is independent when its people are free to rule themselves, instead of being ruled by another country.

Industrializing Building more factories.

Internet A network that allows people all over the world to communicate using computers.

Life expectancy The length of time people can expect to live.

Loom A machine used for weaving cloth.

Manufacturing Turning raw materials into goods for people to use.

Monsoon The wind that brings rain to India.

Plains Large areas of level land.

Planetarium A building where people can find out about the stars and planets, and how they move in the sky.

Plateau An area of high, flat land.

Population The number of people who live in a place.

Raw materials Materials such as wood, metals or chemicals that are used to make goods for people to buy.

Roman Catholics Christians who are led by the Pope, who lives in Rome, Italy.

Shrine A place where religious statues or other objects are kept, around which people gather to pray.

Silicon A natural substance used for making computer chips.

State An area of a country that has its own government.

Taxes Money that people have to pay to the government.

Further information

Books to read

A River Journey: The Ganges by
Rob Bowden (Hodder Wayland, 2003)

Continents: Asia by L. Foster
(Heinemann, 2003)

Festivals and Food: India by Mike Hirst
(Hodder Wayland, 2006)

Living In India by Ruth Thomson
(Franklin Watts, 2002)

Picture a Country: India by
Henry Pluckrose (Franklin Watts, 2001)

The Changing Face Of: India by
David Cumming (Hodder Wayland, 2004)

Traditional Stories from India by Vayu
Naidu (Hodder Wayland, 2006)

Sources

The statistics in this book are from the
following sources:

Manorama Yearbook (Malayala Manorama
Company Ltd.)

CIA World Factbook
(www.cia.gov/cia/publications/
factbook/)

Census India 2001 (www.censusindia.net)

Education For All In India
(www.educationforallinindia.com)

Human Rights Watch (www.hrw.org)

United Nations Development Programme
(www.undp.org)

Virtual Bangalore
(www.virtualbangalore.com)

World Bank (www.worldbank.org)

The website addresses (URLs) included in
this book were valid at the time of going
to press. However, because of the nature
of the Internet, it is possible that some
addresses may have changed, or sites
may have changed or closed down since
publication. While the authors and
publisher regret any inconvenience this
may cause readers, no responsibility for
any such changes can be accepted by
either the authors or the publisher.

Index

Page numbers in **bold** refer to photographs.